Contusions

Jianna Jihyun Park

Contusions ©2019 by **Jianna Jihyun Park**. Published in the United States by Vegetarian Alcoholic Press. Not one part of this work may be reproduced without expressed written consent from the author. For more information, please contact vegalpress@gmail.com

Cover images by **Maggie Haslam**. www.maggiehaslam.com

CONTENTS

THEY PICKED AN ALTHEA FLOWER FROM THIS WOUNDED SOIL.......................5
J'AI DORMI SOUS L'EAU..6
NIRVANA BLUES..7
WHO WATERED THE ROSES ON HER CHEST?..8
MERMAID'S HOWL...9
SUADADES..10
SAUDADES..11
COMPRESSION: 0..12
YOU CRAWLED INTO YOUR VACUUM SEALED BED NAKED.........................13
GERMINATION..14
RE:COGNIZE...15
A DIRGE IN A NEST..16
THE REAL CAUSE OF ADDICTION IS NOT DRUGS, IT'S LONELINESS........17
ESCAPE VELOCITY: A SCRIPT..20
D.S. AL CODA...24
CONFESSIONS I...25
CONFESSIONS II: A PAGEANT..27
EVER WONDERED WHY WE ARE DRAWN TO HIGHER PLACES?...............30
DELECTABLE..31
TOXIN, OXYTOCIN...33
DECATHECT..34
LOVE IS ATTACHMENT BUT ATTACHMENT IS NOT LOVE............................35
CLIFF DIVE..36
A LETTER OF AN APOLOGIST...37
DREAM RELEASE SURRENDER..38
DISTANCE BETWEEN TWO...39
140416..40
SINKHOLE...42
ANGELUS INSOMNUS...44
GENESIS..45
LAST VISIONS OF A BLIND WOMAN...53
L'INCERTITUDE D'HEISENBERG...54
WHAT TO DO WHEN YOUR THROAT IS ITCHY...55

THEY PICKED AN ALTHEA FLOWER FROM THIS WOUNDED SOIL

and dragged me by the pistils that snapped and shed yellow tears they / trampled on the porcelain shards of my / childhood shoeless feet trembled snow / sighing silence over village butterflies / falling from gray sky / like shrapnel / i twitched and danced the dance of dread in their hands for / i cannot speak / i am a flower and i have aphasia // *The only time you can shake your head is when the ashen wind blows from the west smelling steel, bitch, stay still or I'll slap you!* // growing shadows penetrated my / body to dissect my / petals occupied / infected / shredded / screaming sweet / scented water seeped and quenched their thirst against my / uprooted will the flower cringed holding her / aching belly as worn / boots of the soldiers dug bruise-shaped / holes the flower grew weaker she / vomited red unborn baby that was mauled / that howled a long wolf cry for / the young mother a plant / lying on a cold bamboo mat her / tongue / devoured by wrath / breasts consumed / soot-blackened / blood-shot eyes of the unborn / baby they haunt me still / when my / husband beats me with his / breath smelling of soju in the afterhours i / count with deep-cut wrinkles on my / skin don't tell my / daughters what happened in the rice paddies / in the hut / in the pit / among lifeless lumps my / desolate sisters their / pubic hair burnt / unbloomed dreams / inked with blood / who is to say / that tears never dry / ? / mine are scorched salt crystals / stab me from inside until my / hair turns white and falls / who is / to say that freedom / the long-yearned returning home / can free me from these words / left caged between my / gritted / silky / teeth / ?

J'AI DORMI SOUS L'EAU

I just wanted to sleep
Let blue body be my friend

Where did you hide
my fish tear needle?

Hubris is walking
barefoot on your war

debris. I must resist impulse
to count pulse by water

-color crab boy in rotten stomach
Listen to piano howl of whales

Gold fish pull a full moon deep
Slow dive dim moonlight glow

Deathly lively,
or lively death

Opal skeleton says I, C, U
I have a hunch that I'm god

or a bad imitation.
Adieu, bleu—

pale gold flickers
reverberate behind sunken eyes.

NIRVANA BLUES

The moment where the indigo sky turns
to a transparent sheet, with specks of stars and snowflakes
blinking like dusts my mother forgot to vacuum
I lean against the sleepy city to cool my face
or efface it, with a blue airy step off my ninth floor cell.

Broken images tumbling over
and over in my head
since weariness first trickled
down my throat with
the Truth:

But the window only sweats with my crystalized breath
and that's all. No open skull, no concrete blood,
no broken spine but thoughts scurrying away.

Fading streetlights cringe and shiver
but everything remains silent and still
deep down under water where
dawn drags me daily.

I wish I were made of glass
like this window dividing worlds
or perhaps of stainless steel,
if I could be less susceptible to time.

Sometimes, the I inflates like a life vest
and its body forgets how to sink.

When the morning comes, the sun will melt away
the stars and the snowflakes and the frost on my lashes
and my mother will wipe the window with her thumbs
as white and warm as summer daze, and I'll say

it's just insomnia and many must have it.

WHO WATERED THE ROSES ON HER CHEST?

Cold stairs beneath her body, torn ripped polyester legs
Choices sans consent covered in your sweat
Her soil gutted out, roots rooted   She cried for help
in muffled vain. Thorns nibbled her tethered throat
She coughed red, foreign petals on your thick, damp hand.

The night was perspiring like your heavy eyes drooping over
the delicate body folded along dotted line;
oxygen evaporated from her lungs and there since left
stinging ash that puts her into tearless sleep every night
exhaling why—these petals are parched dead in this barren land.

MERMAID'S HOWL
(after Marina Celander)

           dream deferred   (a long haul
temperature of   broken underwater   of *han*)

           blue hue scales   slowly
white silk *hanbok*   slowly appear

lifts   deliberate   of what rejects
    beckons   footing   (was rejected)

whiteness (un)veils   obscures   from within
    encroaches   suffocates   (a cocoon)

fading waves   ripping through   of fond lies
    silent wail   the fabric   of milky memories

stroke ropes   an ocean of   distance
    knots waver (back in time)   is one of silence

which resists to sit still,   burying   unfolded
    resists forgetting   closing—   then strewn

vocal chords   exile, of   elusion   is love
    a documentation of   restless fugitive

is   ash   to chest   breath   by loss.
    from sink   & larynx.   sustained

courage is what it takes   borderless
    to become   water   embrace

mother—   what other name   does clench my   soul , so

SAUDADES

Hugging small legs in the tub, I used to watch
mother cup weary water and submerge her face
leaving a patch of soap on the edge of her temple
that beat softly with the ticking of a clock.

Drops slide along my arms, gathering at elbows
to drip next to my feet. Mirror ripples
permeate my soles like mercurial longing
as I lather a layer of self-assuring lies.

But when warm water erodes my face
I count, bent over a porcelain basin,
how many grams of skin I shed each night
into the drain, gray memories swiveling.

Her water shadows must be crying
My small cupped hands, drowning.

SAUDADES

Hole tells a presence of an absence.

Hole is the rim of your heart that never reaches home

A proof that part of you continues to live somewhere else.

Hole is a place where you sleep beneath a half-written letter, crinkled.

COMPRESSION: 0

The night plane shuddered and jolted
like a shivering wet black dog

Nothing but inert embrace
of the unknown, a relief

Timestamped lights flickered on a wing
Constellations dissolved like sugar grains

The cabin gray, motionless heads escaping in sleep
Reading lights await in REM, then leave one by one

Busy beaded webs of neurons and burnt clouds
of scars floating under the drifting body

Memories are pruned, but not pain
These highways are dense and winding long

Fungi closing in on my brain—
                    here

                            and here

                                          Stop biting nails

                                          Smell of metal
                                          in my crotch

                Fool of yourself, full of yourself

Like landing on a rainy runway
with no gravity, no guiding lights, encircling
in limbo the closing map of the mind
                            misplaced circuit

                                          fused

I grope my brain and pull out
my last pulsing memories and scatter
on the horizon, for this winter's harvest

People gather around dinner table, knifing thin prayers,
moving mouths as if to say something infinite
about this cold, dissolving skin

YOU CRAWLED INTO YOUR VACUUM SEALED BED NAKED

Where you dreamt of drained veins   *
and teeth fallen fractals

There's nothing | you can do   *
To you | there's nothing

How did I lose my   ?

         You scribble
         on dry skin flakes

Was it   *? Should I have been*   *?*

Where you were abandoned   *
you locked the door behind
you, inside you

             White orchids wither and cough

Sorting through a cabinet full of files jagged   *
fingers tap-dance indices of requiem, non-alphabetical order
Grief remains unexcavated, only rising
from time to time like smoke before eruption
hovering, covering your bruised skin
                                      *

Spoon drops—
splattered spleen
fractured bones   *
burning marrow oozes out

                 Not sure what would come out
                 of your open mouth   *
                 Lost words
                 or bubbles
                                                                *

"Elle est malade, comme toutes les femmes avant de dormir."

Burnt papers, words flying aimless,   ash,
                                     ash everywhere.

                                                                          *

GERMINATION

Under the red cotton tree, my body twisted like a snake
Bones crushed, sinews ripped, I screamed but there was no pain.
Nerve cells self-anesthetized   each breath sank
like a silent vessel after a storm. Over my chained body

the red cotton tree shed poisonous blossoms that sealed
my mouth nose eyes and ears. There was no blood,
only tears that soaked the cotton damp and heavy. Atlas kneeled
with the weight of his ego deeper and deeper into the mud.

I forgot how to wake up from the longest dreams
They said my body was a temple of my mind, my mind
but a powerless prey to sly white thoughts that streamed
down bit by bit, crumbling the columns of my shrine.

I saw my rotting body permeate the soil
The branches, beckoning, sprinkled cotton flowers like sleet.

RE:COGNIZE

You say this drains you of life. Lost words of an aphasic—you can't paint when tubes are empty, brush dry—you don't do much. You can't make love. You can't see a child without the crippling guilt, you can't smell a flower but its last dying frenzy. A sharp cut stem sways toeless in deep blue, vegetal, wilted and still. You drop your head into the gutter.

    Excerpts from your diary:

1. *How do you call something whose shape keeps escaping?*
2. *I'm holding a black umbrella under the sun*
3. *I no longer resist sleep paralysis*
4. *My thoughts evaporate into white noise and deafen me inside out*
5. *I read my old diaries and wonder who I was talking to*
6. *I fold summer dresses to never wear them again*
7. *My heart drips water not blood*
8. *The moon breathes cold dim glow into my body*
9. *I smile so I don't spill any of this on you*
10. *I wish to thaw my cheeks but my eyes are melting instead*

What if I told you
fern will grow on your wrist
where you engraved an open letter to me
or
there is blue to your gray
sunrise to your sleep
If your tongue is tied to the back of your mind
paint the clouds with the color of your bruise

(Ringlets of your foreign laughter)

A DIRGE IN A NEST

Waxing and waning
willow tree of silver
Sapphire lake hides in
its depth bemoaning aria

                                        Strings scintillate and vibrate
                                         thinly as if to disappear
                                         flowing away like aurora
                                            frozen memory fading

Souls orbiting like bees around
bedside lilies with rusty pistils
dangling in the remnant of hour
Gravity sheds your mourning hair

                                  Everything that is dying has irresistible
                                  smell imprinted stronger than perfume
                                            like mother's breasts
                                        like fallen leaves rotting

Dawn upon me, impending crash,
looming sister of the moon
Undress me, drag me to your womb
where Eros et Thanatos pulse in sync

                                                  Wedding dress dans le
                                                    danse macabre—
                                                          a moth moans
                                                 luminous attraction

A horse kneels humbly
His muzzle seeks death in hay

THE REAL CAUSE OF ADDICTION IS NOT DRUGS, IT'S LONELINESS

In my dream the land was filled with
methane and I lit my cigarette, all knowing end
The next moment warm brushes of fire
wrapped around me and everything was black

Everything was okay

For what
do you get out of bed every morning?
Deepest connection I ever felt was

I don't have an appetite
I wish to be penetrated
again and again by loss

Black laver hair drapes lunchbox memories
Tiny holes replace yellow collarbone
Blooming body, burning flower
Vines grow in the veins leaking ink

Dry twig powder eyes aloof
Shadow that lost owl light of night

                                        I paint the iris with
                                        forgotten typeface

                    Doves once sang:

                    Water the plant
                      If it withers,
                make it a fertilizer
                    Plant new seed
                    Water the soil
                        Repeat
            until the plant becomes you

Deep water scares me
Bodies that dissipate
remain deep down below my feet

forever buoyant

Every day I wake up underwater

                Leapfrogs once sang:

        On the brink of death, choose not to leap
            – This is not a test –

Bite finger
nails, listen to water head numbing
Bamboo leaves grow from the shower curtain
up the blaring fan

Hair clogs drain again
Pour bleach gel down the hole
Pressures against the tile floor
Diminish as the liquid escapes

                        Nicotine mouth drier than dryads
                           Blazing bush fire of January
                         (I still remember the dream)

           Once said rats:

           Come play with us
           in a cage full of toys
           Choose water
           not war

We used to build sand terrarium without the ceiling
Fist shed time from its ribs and rose
pulverized bones that sat under my nose
Fatigue piled up like dust on grandmother's shelf

                Hana
                Dool
                Set
                Net

Inkjet printer moves back and forth
and asks me if I'm alone

Diamond top spinning capricious
I watch its white hand blades

of grass caressing the mound
where my grandmother sleeps
Once a year they soak incense ash
Nearby pond open zen fish gills

Net
Set
Dool
Hana

and close.

In and out of water are the same
for those who suffocate slow burnt lungs
I wipe her stone slab clean and pluck weeds
learning to fulfill a child's duty

Memories meander through pine tree barks
"Dandelion seeds will extinguish fire."

Just wait,
she said.
Breathe water.

ESCAPE VELOCITY: A SCRIPT
(from *Archive of Lost Things*)

(Film rolls up, then down, then up again
Reeling
                                        stops)

[~~Alcohol abuse~~ is very closely associated with ~~suicide~~ cases in South Korea.]

Father beats mother

You are hiding in your bed, pretending to be asleep
Think of the time your family went to the zoo to see a tiger

Empty green soju bottles roll away on vinyl floor and make small windy noises
Mildew stains grow bit by bit

[Synecdoche, Seoul]

Mother crying, ironing father's button-downs

You are on a swing in a playground
Your neighbor gives you rainbow rice cake
Say thank you
Follow him

[Social isolation is one of the most significant factors that contribute to a number of mental health conditions, including ~~depression~~, ~~addiction~~, ~~hoarding~~ and ~~anxiety~~.]

Dusk

Empty swing swings weakly with the wind

(Film rolls up, then down, then up again
Reeling
      stops

            Frames crisp with dried salt)

[In 2015, about 5.6% of the entire Korean population—about 2 million people—have suffered ~~depression~~ at least once.]

Meet your first love
Give your first everything

He leaves, paralyzed with fear

You will bear the burden of your love for the rest of your life

(Rub your protruding belly counter-clockwise)

[Fundamental error]

What would solipsists think of each other?

[A novel I Have the Right to Destroy Myself *by Young-Ha Kim was published in 1996.]*

Choose not to destroy your (his) baby
The world is sinking slowly
Name your daughter after the sky
You can see it shifting from underwater

(Film rolls up, then down, then up again
Reeling
                stops

                                  Frames burnt on the edge)

[58.3% of ~~suicides~~ from 1996 to 2005 used pesticide poisoning as South Korean law heavily restricts firearms possession.]

Meet someone who makes you hope
He brings birthday cake for your daughter

An airplane slow-cuts the sky
Smoke trail burns your lungs

Remember gravity, how it holds everything close to the origin

[   ]

Another abandon

[Talking openly about mental illness is still ~~taboo~~ in South Korean society.]

Tell people the sky is too bright to look at
They tell you it's your fault

[South Korea has one of the highest ~~suicide~~ rates among OECD member countries. ~~Suicide~~ is the number one cause of death for South Korean teenagers.]

Walk down the bridge on a windy day
See a phone booth with a sign

The sky opens, and closes, and opens again
Ash flickers into water

It'll seem small and far away
It'll seem small and far away

Keep on walking, despite it all

D.S. AL CODA

I wished you'd go away, you
woke up next to a lightning-stricken tree
where you came back to me, over and over

On the brink of your death you saw
a vision of the world from the gutters, hell,
I wished you'd go away. Your

glistening lips, are you listening? You
wore a laurel crown on a cold winter night
you turned your back to me. Over

the leaves, bag of your longing
morning glory blooms like bullet-
fountain hands creeping up your skirt

Lie in a fir bed I made for you, let
whispering critters enter your caves
Just like that, how I wished it'd go away

Tourmaline eyes pulse through hollow crowds. Fall,
fall—the moon shatters, each shard an image of your fear
I thought I wished you'd go away until
I turned your body over.

CONFESSIONS I

One.

"Beyond the abyss lies the light"

I'm walking up the limestone stairs, no, I'm climbing, hardly catching breath. No, I don't want you to chase after me, my blue dream tentacles. The world is flooded as always in my swollen sleep. The water is rising and I'm tired of breathing. I'm tired of this growing heat, my lungs perspire and I'm already drowning inside me. Purge me. Every step stares back at me as if asking where I'm going. These stairs are slowly eroding. Calcite bubbles pull my ankles with their tiny hands.

Two.

Night falls like wine stain. Clouds cover clotted blood. Underneath the tranquil lake hides a fluther of memories, drifting flashlights.

Three.

"Beyond the abyss—"

Our apartment drowned. Our nine years old Maltese drowned. My thoughts of you drowned as your soft singing voice drowned. You might as well have been sobbing. The only thing that didn't drown is a pair of sneakers I left on the bridge. They begged to stay. You're safe to walk away in them. I forgot to unclog our shower drain and now you don't know what to do with the gel in your hand.

Four.

Laver hair drips black water   drip

                              drip

                 drip

                                    drip

                                                    drip

Five.

"...lies the light"

And we are drawn to it. You said drowning was the way to go. You didn't say it stings like jellyfish, poisonous voltage. Brain gasping, eyes dilated, eardrums bursting kaleidoscopes, I waited for the last relief.

Electrified—I waited.

Six.

A blue jellyfish inhales; water gravitates toward the marred heart
She coughs out a black hairball before floating away

The bridge collapses, slow dives into the abyss

CONFESSIONS II: A PAGEANT

    BLUE DREAM TENTACLES
Contusions grow from my body. They are made for you, my dear child. Embrace me.

    BLACK LAVER HAIR
Embrace, you.

    GRAY HOURS
        (drip)   (drip)   (drip)

    BLUE DREAM TENTACLES
I am mere a shadow, but I am real. I grow and live by you, like algae on a sunken ship.

    GRAY HOURS
        I grow on you

    A PAIR OF SNEAKERS
I'm also real, but I'm not a shadow. Run with me, you'll remember. You're bleeding. Salt crystals are stabbing you.

    BLACK LAVER HAIR
Don't, remember, anything. Hold, breath, my. Devour me, Gray Hours.

    A PAIR OF SNEAKERS
Turn around and follow the singing voice. I'll comb you with my noses and wipe your tears with the laces.

BLACK LAVER HAIR
Too wet, heavy, this. Tired. One last, leap, wish.

GRAY HOURS
You deserve it

A PAIR OF SNEAKERS
Hush.

BLACK LAVER HAIR
Clogged, I feel, I am. Vanish, longing. More, is there? Drain my blood.

GRAY HOURS
Maybe, maybe, maybe…

BLUE DREAM TENTACLES
Come into this tunnel, sweetie, I made it for you. Sleep here in peace, nothing can wake you. Let me caress your swollen limbs. Lullaby is sweet oblivion.

A PAIR OF SNEAKERS
Remember the faces—your wounds will heal.

GRAY HOURS & A PAIR OF SNEAKERS
You're braver than you think.

BLACK LAVER HAIR
Drain me I drain I purge my—

BLUE DREAM TENTACLES
The flight is yours. I am here to catch you. Do not worry.

GRAY HOURS
                        The water is yours

        A PAIR OF SNEAKERS
Tomorrow is yours. Just wait. Breathe.

EVER WONDERED WHY WE ARE DRAWN TO HIGHER PLACES?
(in *Archive of Lost Things*)

1. The number of cells in multicellular organisms is tightly regulated. If cells are no longer needed, they commit suicide by activating a programmed cell death, called apoptosis. The word comes from a Greek word meaning "falling off," as leaves falling from a tree. Between 50 and 70 billion cells die each day due to apoptosis in the average human adult. For an average child between the ages of 8 and 14, approximately 20 billion to 30 billion cells die a day.

2. Globally, an estimated 350 million people of all ages suffer from depression. If people feel they are no longer needed, they commit suicide that is either premeditated or spontaneous. In South Korea, on average, one person commits suicide every 37 minutes. About two thirds of people who complete suicide are depressed at the time of their deaths. Depression that is untreated, undiagnosed, or ineffectively treated is the number one cause of suicide.

3. Cells that die as a result of acute injury typically swell and burst. They spill their contents all over their neighbors—a process called cell necrosis—causing a potentially damaging inflammatory response. By contrast, a cell that undergoes apoptosis dies neatly, without damaging its neighbors. The cell shrinks and condenses. The cytoskeleton collapses, the nuclear envelope disassembles, and the nuclear DNA breaks up into fragments. Most importantly, the cell surface is altered, displaying properties that cause the dying cell to be rapidly phagocytosed, either by a neighboring cell or by a macrophage, before any leakage of its contents occurs.

4. When you hit water, your body went from 75 mph to nearly zero in a nanosecond. The force of the impact severely damaged your internal organs. Autopsy reports indicate that your stomach, liver, and heart are torn loose. Ribs are broken and are sharply shoved deep into your nicotine lungs. You also have a fractured skull and broken clavicle. You chose to shrink and condense the last weeks of your life so as not to be seen. Contrary to what you believed, your suicide affects at least six other people that were close to you. Your mother and sister stop eating. Your letter headlines a local newspaper. Then, like everything else, it is soon forgotten.

5. Apoptosis can be initiated through one of two pathways. In the intrinsic pathway, the cell kills itself because it senses cell stress. In the extrinsic pathway, the cell kills itself when it gets signals from other cells.

6. Suicide chain effect brings young copycats to the bridge you left behind. Red headlights are swarming underneath. People install phone booths that say "life line." They wait for a call.

DELECTABLE

I scalded my hand the other day, boiling spinach,
squeezing life out of wrinkled bodies
holding an ice bag now limp, I told myself
I should let go of this.

                    (I remembered the brush of pressurized steam
                    jetting out of a finished rice cooker, the water
                    distilled to throbbing blisters on my fingers;
                    or the temperature of iron that smoothed out
                    white linen while my wrist hid words in welts)

& rub salt off my eyes—it's already late, there is so
much work to do and a fish I got on sale yesterday.
stainless steel sharpened to obsession
grab the tail, remove the scales by stroking
in the opposite direction of their making

                    (I used to watch my mother at work and collect
                    iridescent flakes that scattered all over the sink,
                    daydreaming about pearls, urchins and mermaids)

trim off the fins and tail
behead the soundless weight with one quick conclusion

                    (my father liked the cheeks but I do not wish
                    to see its white eyes opaque with the realization of the
                    body
                    transforming in fire, its mouth agape, paralyzed)

then under cold running water rinse the head-
-less lump that is naked, slippery and gleaming like tongue.
the oil waits silently before swallowing
with garlic, onion, chili and ginger whose screams I cover
with lid until they become murmur. think I've given enough
time; serve it on a blue plate, garnish with lime and cilantro.
chopsticks break open the flesh exhaling the last steam
and lift a mouthful when I see a fingernail,
not clipped but whole, scorched black like soot
still attached to a finger. the temperature
drop—

i look into the garbage and see
my head staring up at me
with its white bleeding eyes.

TOXIN, OXYTOCIN

I wear a well-ironed cotton blouse
to show you my good intentions
I baked cupcakes for you, acidic heart sprinkles on top

Under neon motel sign we counted blessings
in a matchbox. Phosphorus snow fell and glowed
on our foreheads when you said it'd be okay

Questions are corrosive, a deadly venom that tethers
to my hollow and you are standing too close. When
dendrites tickle my brain with blue serotonin

I don't know any other way. Look at me
with loving contempt, don't mind the smell of sulfur
that won't disappear with these lies

Now I have a fever and I'm hungry for your anger
I drink from your patience until water turns rock
My chest is burning, looking for a false reward

Tell me I'm not adequate. I beg you to pardon
and abandon me. Stomp on my stomach, spit on my face
leave me with a relief of knowing that you're safe

    Someone said not to play with fire
for it can burn your most cherished object

I wanted to show you how I die
so you'd die inside too

Red plastic hole expands
and falls black bile on the motel floor

DECATHECT

I pick a grain of sticky rice
A thread crawls out of my sweater

Boil me a cup of dandelion
Pour a sachet of resignation
And stir, so I can smell and sip
My secret little melancholy

My idea of you
Lives before you

Outside the train window
You're walking toward me
But growing smaller, farther
Away from my plastic seat

I listen to your breath
My ear to your chest

Like a quiet conch
Holding onto an ocean rock
That is soon to be washed
Away by a gushing storm

You're sitting in front of me
But you're already gone

The imprint of your smile
Mere an afterimage, an echo
Reverberating around
Unfinished bittersweet tea

LOVE IS ATTACHMENT BUT ATTACHMENT IS NOT LOVE

I cannot wear a wool sweater without a layer underneath
My chest soon blooms with red moss I itch to water

just like when I wore a fake necklace that turned
lichen as I sweat a mouthful of lies

It doesn't matter, for example—
it matters as much as it matters to me

how many people to whom you said I love you before
or when I picked up a foreign strand of hair off your pillow

and drained it down the shower as I scalded my body
(I scolded it for imitating the temperature of your body)

As much as you say I am sensitive and that's what you love
about me, I am sensitive to the ribcage that it breaks

into multitudes of sharp shreds
and fall scattering loose

when I see a chiaroscuro of your face
turning away from mine

The weight of silence sliced slant
bleeding memory between us

I want to be your veins
flow our memories in your sleep

raise temperature to a boil
so you ache in my thoughts

CLIFF DIVE

You said the bruises would go away in three days, that you well know this kind
but it's been two weeks since and it is you that's gone now, not these
purple and yellow fingerprints all over my body when the water hit me falling from 50ft high
They linger, how I gasped for a breath of air (have you ever swallowed void, empty stomach
is not empty until everything is vacuumed out tight)
how I shivered and you never once held me right
how you and I caught a bad cold afterwards, and when we recovered
we decided to recover from each other as well.

Momentum outgrows time as memories
like falling loose, then fades
I still wonder, *if I never came back, would you have cried*
Would you have realized how far I could go for you

It's been slightly more than a month now and the bruises are gone too
Just a small scar tissue nodule under the skin inside my shin
I run my fingers along the cave of my bone, to feel the lump
to see if the bruises left me any other trace of you, knotted.

A LETTER OF AN APOLOGIST

Solitude sounds close to the grinding of an almond between my teeth. Dry, hard, mouth-cottoning, leaving pieces behind the tongue like words almost forgotten. You said your default belief was knowing you are all alone. Tell me, how do you move on from that. How do you untrust yourself in order to trust someone else over and over. You think I am a flower, the reason for your being. I continue to fail. It is not from some outside source; it is I who choose to trample on myself. You pick up a trampled flower and put it in your vase. How long will you look at it. Why do I give you a trampled flower. I want to give you a nice, fresh flower. You have cuts on your hands from my thorns. I do not wish to be a rose. I want to be water. Or a rescue dog. Something that forgets itself. Something that forgives to embrace you. It licks your wounded hands. You said you still find yourself dead in a bathtub sometimes. If I were water I would turn red and find a way back into your veins. Right now I am a pool of still water and I am lost in myself. I smell putrid. You still want to drink me, knowing you will get sick. I do not want to make you sick, I want you to bloom. I disappear into the soil. I leave rotten petals and carcasses behind. I drip underneath and slip into a stream where you can dip your feet. With words you make the air big and hot, I am lifted. To show gratitude I plunge into your skin in millions of molecules. Like that, I am one with your tears. Like that, I want to be absorbed back into you.

DREAM RELEASE SURRENDER

Our kiss turns into suffocation as your slippery tongue grows larger and larger in my mouth. You are now a one-eyed serpent and you begin to constrict me with your body coiling around my torso. My torso shrinks, ribcage and spine wrapped within immense pressure. I struggle to push away from you by leaning backward, to escape, to protect what little space I have left, but the more I resist the more unbearable the pain grows. My tight spine feels as if it's about to snap. It is similar to the fear of dislocating the kneecap while trying to walk with a numb leg after a long sitting, right before fiery needles of blood return and slowly circulate autonomy. Your eye is too close to mine I cannot see anymore. Then, I let go. I abandon resistance. I think of surrendering to you in any way you wish, and at that moment, I no longer fear anything. I think I understand why, because as soon as my body loosens, you release the hold. Your trace slips away from me like draining water, and my spine repositions as my eyes open and slowly adjust to the dark ceiling of my room. My body sinks back into the mattress, suddenly remembering how to breathe. The muscles in my back still throb from the remnant of sensations. Silence reverberates in my ears. The sheet is damp with sweat. Amidst static chaos, I find relief—my bosom is full as a wall of morning glories, my love for you the sun.

DISTANCE BETWEEN TWO

Sori (sound)
Mok-sori (throat-sound; voice)
Neo'ae papyeondle (pieces of you)

Dissect, disintegrate, recollect, reinvent
shapes and sounds of our bodies
that collide and leave
soft blue scars

It is perpendicular, not parallel
(but you were the only thing I
remembered when I was lost)

Sori: sound. Under the roof by a river, of which the composition is you. A coffee table in the kitchen, a white orchid remembering the sunlight avalanching from the tip of your head. You said something to me in French, I said something to you in English. I wanted to kiss you in Korean. The tongue withdraws and the silent image of you staring at the white orchid plays over and over in my head.

Neo: you. The tongue pushes the ceiling gently to make room for your breath to enter. An angle of space, reaching for a doorknob, then a crossing of space: two lines grow toward each other, heading north east and north west—after the brief encounter (singular), the lines continue on their paths. Tails of two particles.

Papyeon: pieces, scraps of something which is broken, usually from an impact or explosion. A square form is broken, from an explosion inside of you. An atom dismantling, gravity lost. Half-life of passion. (The energy remains the same, it just flows somewhere else; you are the entropy, a living decay.)

140416

1:45

Black clothes hanging,
vacant and heavy—
swollen, unnamed bodies
dream of returning home

Head ringing with clamor
I close my eyes
and open
Time stops ticking

The clothes lift their arms

10:17

What was it like
to embrace a cold body
of water deep blue
creeping up on you

Cringing, creaking vessel
Howl of the sirens
no one could hear
but the children
"Do not come out,
I repeat
Do not move."
So they obeyed, scared but tame
clinging onto one last breath

They waited.

Broken nails
Scratches on slippery walls
Rest bed for grieving algae

Do not breathe in,
or your lungs will freeze

295

The night was too long, for every waiting hand
I heard the diver holding flashlight
cried underwater
Straps of vests tied together
Some were found, never to be found again

Candlelight glow like bones
The ones left behind arrange framed portraits of tomorrow

9

Blackboard filled with white names,
White flowers grow on wooden desks.
April sky is clear and blue
Golden ribbons adorn tree boughs
I wanted to be a tree, standing tall and kind
but my leaves have lost their green.
My trunk shrinks and withers
Salty sap keeps oozing out
Where did you go, my friends?
It's time for class, but the teacher's gone
and the chairs are empty, too.
Where did you go, kids?
Where did you go?

SINKHOLE

what if
  not feeling
is not
  sensory deprivation

                what indicates
                you're
                          (not)
                  alone?

  childhood
      zero
gravity
  (your)
          narrow echoes
shadow
      marrow
  of colors

tunnel   vision
        (vide)

        ink
          dive
        on the brink
          of
  spit e

      o
hum ming
      ( )

                    around
              &&
with in
      au
      dessous

  pitch
      black
      radius
  deep
beneath   this

```
                        cluster
                                    (phobic)
cauchemar
  (you called me)
            clandestine


                    pit     ch
    (no sound)
blind
            sighting

                vacuum

devour
            hour
              people
            cars
              trees
            houses


(our)
            pas
(breath)


                        better off
                        without
    (no      pain)

anatomy
  of   dis integration


                                open
            stomach
                        warm
to touch
(to touch
            in spite of)

itch
wish            (t here)



            look


                        up
```

ANGELUS INSOMNUS

Black. Blue. Maybe white—no, ~~white noise~~ gray. Gray. Stable. ~~grave gravity gravel~~ Static dusts ~~periwinkle~~ twinkle in my eyes. Perish one by one ~~by one by one~~. Silent. …Silence. —— (Science says) Head ringing ~~((((ring ring ring ring ring))))~~ Like how it would be in the space. Vacuu~~uuuuu~~m. Empty (no one). Chamomile honey ~~yellowish gray~~ aroma in the room lingers ~~world loses chroma at 3:45am.~~ Heavy, dense (has ever died) black curtain of hair | | | | | | | from (from) above. She is asleep ~~she whispers inaudible words in her sleep~~ but I'm not (insomnia). Her arms are crossed under ~~above~~ her meager breasts, in a way you do when you're cold ~~bats are warm bloodied mammals~~. Stone gray feet ~~upside down~~ rooted in the ceiling ~~downside up~~ a slab of body hanging (Deprivation of sleep). Ribs are (has been) protruded (widely) casting deep lines of shadow ~~my eye bags~~ under mammalian moonlight. ~~Is she me is me her~~ Lying still, stare ~~stairs Altair all tear up~~ at her diaphanous webbed wings (used as)— bluish gray (a means of) grayish black—silky muted ~~please~~ down velvet vein (torture) ~~let me~~ one two three four five six feet ~~underwater~~ long half open, half closed, no breeze, tactile death ~~tick tock tick tock~~ don't know how much time elapsed ~~relapse elongated time lapse~~ her face is calm sea ~~sheepless sleep sleepless sheep~~ it tides in ~~t i c k   t o c k~~ absorbs my sleep, tides out ~~t i c k   t o c k~~ exhales salt air it reddens my eyes ~~t   i   c   k   t   o   c   k~~ drab ambience ~~turtle reach for Ambien in a gray bottle~~ makes me drown in drowsiness again I wait ~~in a blue black bottle d   r   o   w   n   i   n   g~~

_____
_____
_____am I hallucinating .

GENESIS

Fish is the proto-human, our first ancestor.

***

I believed I would find out the truth of the universe before I turned 26.
I also believed I would   when I turned 26.

It's like you wish to want to fuck but you never get wet. Pleasurable is a world away and you can only observe it from this side of the window. Your mind is drooling not because of desire but because you're paralyzed.

What does it feel like—the end of a carbon pencil after writing the same thing over and over? (Dull, worn, fatigued)

Reindeer are the only species of deer among which females also grow antlers. But in a stressful environment, antlerless females can be spotted.

***

Act I

Hand. Cut. Saw. Back
and forth. Repeat.
Grow. Plant. Consume.
Inhale. Run. Stop.
Hide. White tail flinch.

***

Setting: cold, gray, square room. A metal frame bed and a surveillance camera.

This is a longitudinal study, closure indefinite

                                                                  like your sorrow

Dependent Variable: Your will has never been free

Sample Size: $N = 1$

Let's begin an experiment.
On what conditions can we develop a disorder?

***

Day 1

~~I~~ They put me in a room, I don't know ~~where~~ the name of this play
There is a door ~~I don't know if~~ I can walk out through

~~I remember feeling sad~~ I don't remember much about my childhood
I was always tired

There's salt water in a cup
I'm waiting
                                        for the dread to wake

Repeat after me: I know it all.
               There is no way out.

                        I will put a plenty of butterflies in your cage

Day 2

(Resistance; intermittent sobbing)

~~I can't tell~~ the room is gray white or black
Wish to get out of here but ~~better stay~~ don't know how

Day 3

Or who I should go to
They might be ~~thinking I'm a burden~~ busy

Butterflies stopped flying
Wings tap on the steel bars, embracing the cold

Stillness doesn't bother me

Day 7

(Collateral symptoms)

I bend over a white pool of water
The stomach twitches
Acidic smell and throat pain

Wash the tip of the brush
Water runs
A tooth rolls down the sink

Day 35

(Conditioning)

Black dog appeared
He is tied in a corner of the room
Drools, eyes whine
I sit beside him, let him lap my hand (a warm, wet tongue)

When the bell disappears I think of my first kiss (a warm, wet tongue)

Day 38

They took him away
in a cold apatite cage

Leaving me with
this absence

Day 58

People in the TV say
"   "
Not enough nonchalance

I pluck my hair out
Braid them into a rope

They take it away too

Day 100

Repeat after me: I am nothing / I am nothing / am nothing / nothing

Through the TV they talk to me
Sometimes I respond
When I do they can't hear because
either they're inside the box
or I'm inside the box

It is clear no one can hear my words

Day 124

Dream of a vast meadow with wild flowers
At night it turns into a reservoir of hailing comets

You appeared
You are grazing on wild flowers
Your antlers are big and strong, fully adorned with stardust
We gallop in the field, listening to faraway waves

Day 149

Heard a song in my head
It goes like

Saw-cut your antlers
They are your thoughts
Peel the bark
Eat them raw
Blood smiles
la la la la la

and recedes

Day 158

Started shedding

Day 196

Real mermaids don't have any hair

How does their tail taste like?
How fast do they crawl?

Day 207

(Stabilized)

Scratched scalp all day
Unbearable itch
Scabs fell from body and formed a mound

Pain escapes me

Day 266

(No specificity)

        If I weren't there
                would it all have been better
                              ?

***

Act II

Slide. Slip. Sleep. Open.
Sleep. Slit. Stare. Sleep.
Breathe. Sleep. Dream.
Forget.

***

They relocated me to another room. There's a swimming pool in the middle. Nauseating smell of chlorine and carcasses. Antlers stopped growing, like everything else.

Day 570

Rubbing alcohol on my head
My thoughts sterilize
Evaporate

Day 613

(Viscosity of skin)

Day 701

(Fins grow
Fingers web)

Day 799

(Gills appear)

Hard to breathe
My thorax filled with water

Day 817

(   )

Day 900

(Time to swim)

Day 999

Stars collide
No one knows
What shapes you take
Underwater

(A leaking heart)

***

Day 1

This is a longitudinal study, closure indefinite

LAST VISIONS OF A BLIND WOMAN

Trapped inside
I hear your voice

Touch me
I'm shedding my skin

Put your hand behind a book
Is the hand still there?

Quieting dawn in the frozen hours
Just a haze, without destination

Topography of consciousness:
anchored but flexible, as if dog bitten

A baseball glance follows
wringing tail the depth of your bearing

Curves flowing fast like heated motors
past me inside and in front of

Vacillating pareidolia
Your recognition is heavenly

"Isolation is delusion of separate self,
compassion will enable to suffer with"

How long is forever?
Sometimes bedrock, sometimes a word

Everyone's trying their best
and it makes me want to cry

L'INCERTITUDE D'HEISENBERG

Wet night soil brings me back in time
where I hid myself under the dark of a bridge

Smell of burnt cedar
Soft cushions of hay grass

Silver in rain glistening on each glimpse of
blade. To the mother of pearl sky

one might wonder
if this is infinity.

Driving toward the sunset
when beads of rain on windshield

become yellow diamonds,
streaks of trickling time.

Rituals—the peculiarity of
a halo on a sleepy boy's hair

It is difficult to excise the physical
You won't let others mourn death but your own

WHAT TO DO WHEN YOUR THROAT IS ITCHY

I pluck seed leaves from a pine cone
one by one with my fingernails.
Brittle drops of tear dry into sheer
dragonfly wings with hummingbird eyes
sighing and dying, dying to be born again.
The yarns of their ligaments and veins
are golden streams threading
the geography of your folds.

Conifers whisper: *you split open to grow a sage from within.*
Round and round falls a wooden petal.

It is easy to forget that mountains care and that
pine trees, bent from the years of gusts and snow
and the hefty heat of blazing summers until
they stand stout, head pointing skyward, care

NOTES

"They Picked an Althea Flower from this Wounded Soil" is for "comfort women" who were forced into sexual slavery during WWII.

The italicized line in "Nirvana Blues" is after Ernest Hemingway's "A Clean, Well-Lighted Place."

"A Dirge in a Nest" is after Lars von Trier's film *Melancholia* (2011) and Tchaikovsky's "Autumn Song."

Most lines of "Ever Wondered Why We Are Drawn to Higher Places?" were found on Wikipedia, NIH, and SF Gate.

"140416" is for the victims of the Sewol Ferry incident that took place on April 16, 2014 in South Korea.

ACKNOWLEDGEMENTS

"Confessions I" and "Angelus Insomnus" appeared in *Aisthesis*.

"Decathect" appeared in Z Publishing's *Indiana's Best Emerging Poets*.

"Love is Attachment but Attachment is not Love" appeared in *The Juggler*.

I would like to thank all of you who encouraged me to stay honest to myself.

www.ingramcontent.com/pod-product-compliance
Lightning Source LLC
Chambersburg PA
CBHW060507080526
44584CB00015B/1579